HOW THINGS HAVE CHANGED

Holidays

JON RICHARDS

Chrysalis Children's Books

First published in the UK in 2004 by
Chrysalis Children's Books
An imprint of Chrysalis Books Group Plc
The Chrysalis Building, Bramley Road,
London W10 6SP

ISBN 1 84458 163 2

British Library Cataloguing in Publication Data for this book is available from the British Library.

Editorial Manager *Joyce Bentley*
Editorial Assistant *Camilla Lloyd*
Produced by Tall Tree Ltd
Designer *Ed Simkins*
Editor *Kate Simkins*
Consultant *Jon Kirkwood*
Picture Researcher *Lorna Ainger*

Printed in China

Some of the more unfamiliar words used in this book are explained in the glossary on page 31.

Typography *Natascha Frensch*
Read Regular, READ SMALLCAPS and Read Space;
European Community Design Registration 2003 and
Copyright © Natascha Frensch 2001-2004
Read Medium, Read Black and *Read Slanted*
Copyright © Natascha Frensch 2003-2004

READ™ is a revolutionary new typeface that will enchance children's understanding through clear, easily recognisable character shapes. With its evenly spaced and carefully designed characters, READ™ will help children at all stages to improve their literacy skills, and is ideal for young readers, reluctant readers and especially children with dyslexia.

Photo Credits:
The publishers would like to thank the following for their kind permission to reproduce the photographs:

Lorna Ainger: 1, 2, 11t, 27t (models: Karen Costelloe, Joanne Coggin), 27b, 28b, 29br, bl **Alamy:** Bananastock 25b, 29tr, Steve Davey/La Belle Aurore 5b, Chad Ehlers 5t, Robert Harding World Imagery 14, Chris Howes/Wild Places Photography 15t, Neil Setchfield 7l, BC, S.T. Yiap 8, FCc **The Art Archive:** Musee du Louvre Paris/ Dagli Orti 10 **Photo courtesy of BUNAC Travel Services Ltd.:** 12 **Courtesy Center Parcs:** 13b, 29tl, 31 **Reproduced by kind permission of Thomas Cook UK Ltd.:** 9b, 28t **Corbis:** Mimmo Jodice 6, Fctl, David Lees 4, Hal Lott 19t, Alen MacWeeney 19b, Frances G. Mayer 7r **Courtesy Cunard:** 17b **Getty Images:** AFP 23t, Tim Boyle 23b, General Photographic Agency 20, A. Hudson 22, Hulton Archive 18, Kean Collection 26t, Edward G. Malindine 16, FCbr **Courtesy Hunter Hotels, Plettenberg Bay, R.S.A.:** 15b **The Morphy Richards Orbit Travel Iron:** 25t **Robert Opie:** 24, FCtr **Courtesy Swift Motor Homes:** 21 t, b, FCbl **Tall Tree Ltd.:** 9t, 11b, 17t, 26b, 29c, 30 **The Satellite large family sized tent from Wynnster Outdoor Leisure:** 13t

Contents

Festival days

Holidays began as special days to celebrate religious festivals – the word 'holiday' comes from the phrase 'holy day'. Today, a holiday is a period of time that people take off from work or school to rest, travel or have fun.

People in Ancient Egypt were allowed 70 days off each year for religious festivals, while the Romans had more than 100 holidays to celebrate their gods. Pilgrimages, in which a person travelled to a holy site to worship, were another form of religious break. Many pilgrimages are still undertaken today. One of these is the *Hajj*, the Muslim pilgrimage to Mecca in Saudi Arabia.

◀ This medieval carving shows people on a Christian pilgrimage. Popular Christian destinations include Rome and Jerusalem.

◀ In 17th-century Germany, people started to bring trees into their houses and decorate them for the Christmas holidays.

As important events occurred, people took time off to celebrate them and the people these were associated with. Martin Luther King Day in the US is a popular example, as is Republic Day in India, which commemorates the start of the Indian Republic in 1950.

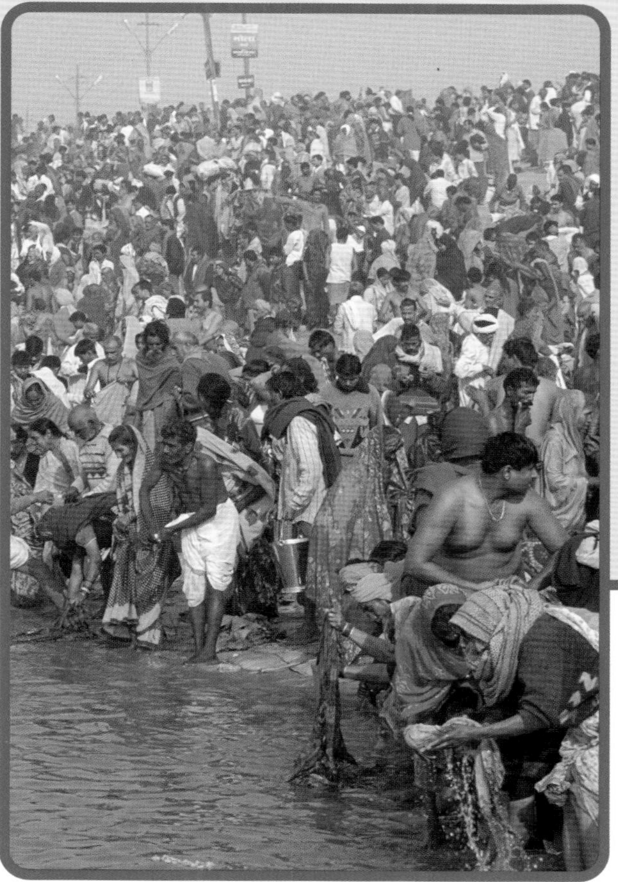

LOOK CLOSER

Kumbh Mela is a Hindu pilgrimage to rivers in India. Pilgrims bathe in the rivers to clean their bodies and souls. Some 20 million people make this pilgrimage every year, making it the largest religious gathering in the world.

Long breaks

The first long holidays were taken by wealthy Romans, who went to their villas to escape the city in the hot summer. Improved travel has allowed more people to take long breaks and to experience different cultures.

Many Roman villas were built around pools of water, which would help to keep the houses cool in summer. This was in contrast to the densely packed streets of the cities that would be unbearably hot at this time.

► **This painting shows a Roman villa. The Emperor Hadrian (AD 117–138) had a villa in Tivoli, Italy, that was surrounded by exotic gardens.**

LOOK CLOSER

From the mid-16th century, young, rich men from England were sent around Europe in the company of a tutor to improve their education. This holiday became known as the Grand Tour. Popular cities on the tour were Paris and Rome. In this painting, tourists are visiting the Pantheon in Rome.

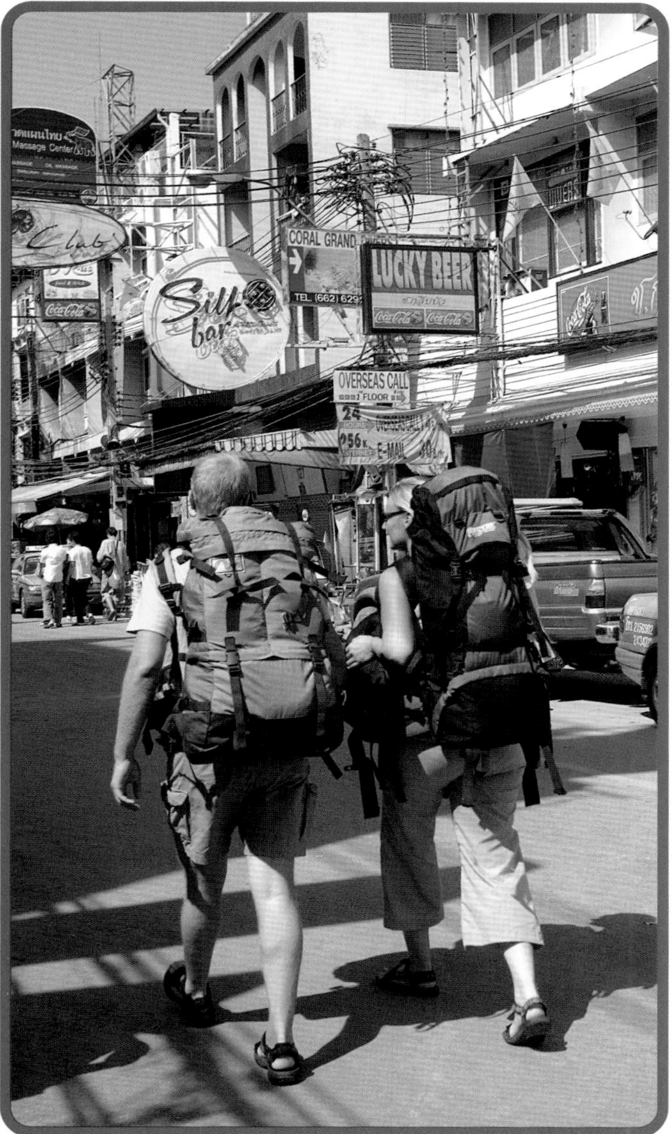

Due to the development of cheap travel today, far more people are able to visit other countries. One popular form of long holiday is 'backpacking', which is an inexpensive break where people travel with backpacks and stay in budget hostels around the world.

◀ **Many young people go backpacking in the gap year between school and university.**

Short breaks

Some holidays may last just a few days or two to three weeks. These short breaks were not affordable to all at first, but they soon became popular, helped by the introduction of a new kind of holiday – the package holiday.

The South Metropolitan Gas Company of Britain was one of the first companies to give its workers paid holidays in 1871. Paid holidays meant that families could afford to take short breaks. Initially, these were taken in resorts that were near to home as travel was still expensive.

▼ Beach holidays are a favourite destination for a short break. People are attracted by the good weather and the experience of visiting a foreign country.

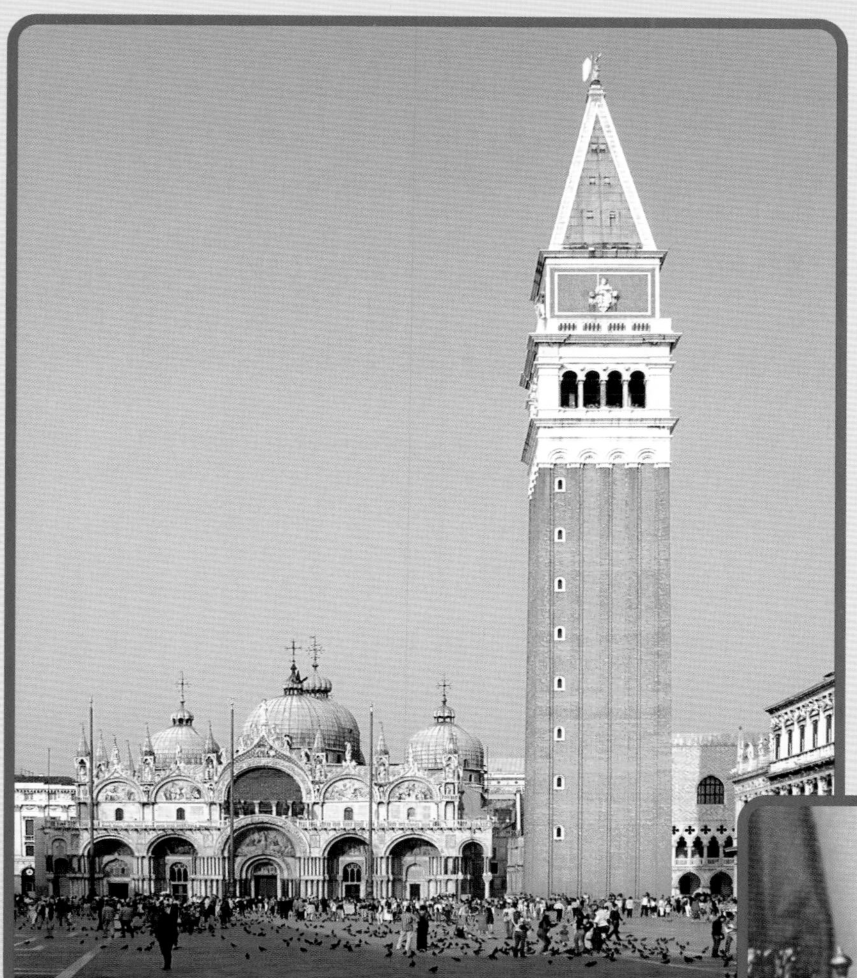

▲ **Weekend breaks to cities such as Venice have been made more popular in recent years due to the availability of cheap flights.**

The introduction of package holidays and the reduction in the cost of travel after World War II (1939–45) created a boom in short breaks to foreign countries. Today, for example, more than 75 million people travel to France every year, making it the world's most popular tourist destination.

EUREKA!

In 1841, Thomas Cook organised a day trip from Leicester to Loughborough, UK, and established the world's first travel agency. When he died in 1892, the Thomas Cook agency was the largest in the world.

Places to stay

People need a place to stay when they go away. The first accommodation for travellers were inns along a road. Later came luxury hotels, boarding houses and motels.

The Ancient Persians, whose empire flourished over 2500 years ago, built small inns along their roads called *caravanserais*, and the Romans had small hotels called *mansionis*. In the Middle Ages, travellers could stay in monasteries along the way.

▼ Travelling by coach in the 18th century took a long time. Coach houses were set up along routes so that people could rest, eat and sleep, and the horses could be changed.

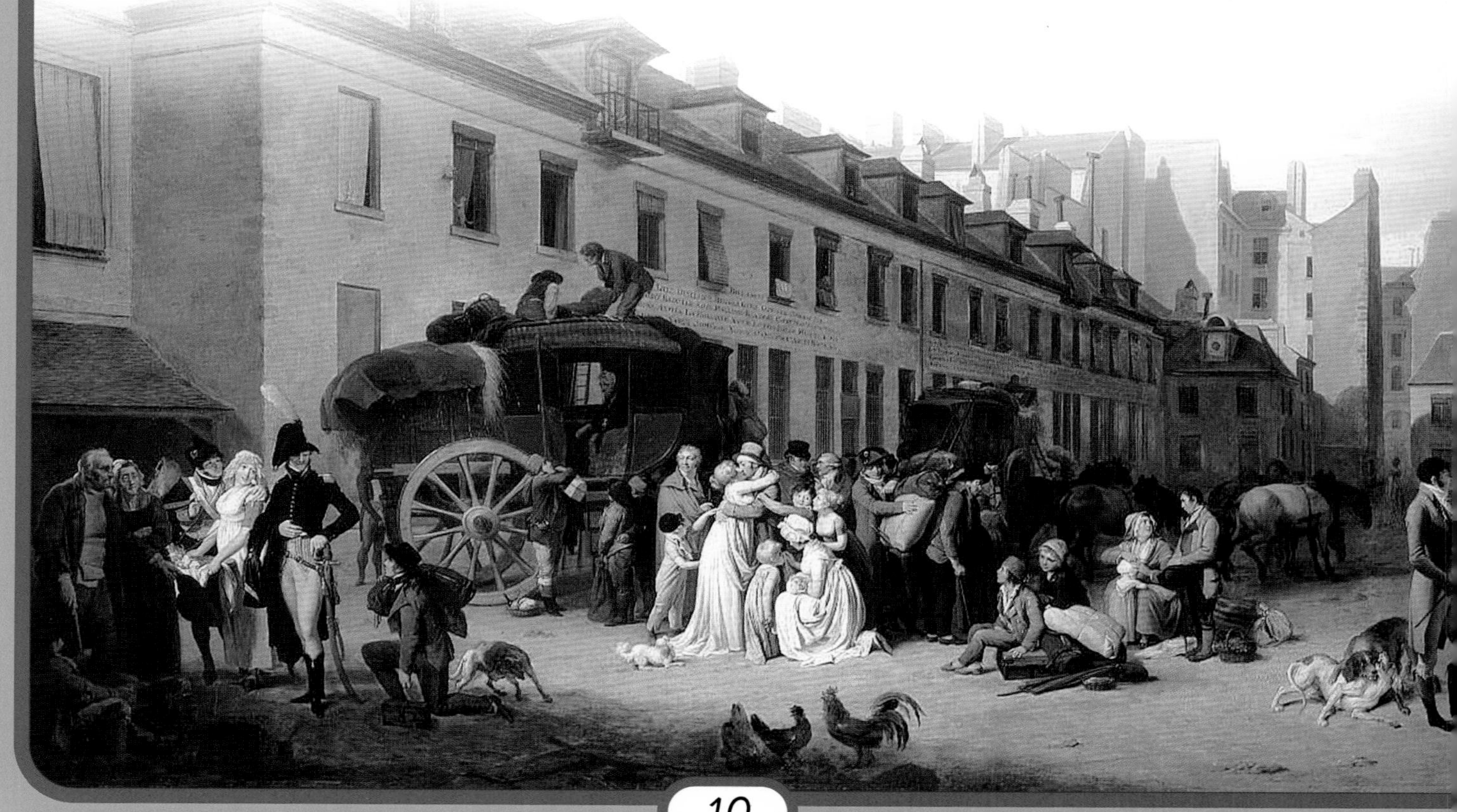

EUREKA!

American Kemmons Wilson revolutionised the hotel industry when he opened his first Holiday Inn in Memphis, USA, in 1952. Wilson's idea was to offer travellers a reliable standard of affordable accommodation. Previously, hotels varied greatly in standards and price. Within 25 years, there were 1700 Holiday Inns around the world.

Rail travel arrived in the 19th century and with it came the first large-scale hotels. Today, massive hotels are built to cater for huge numbers of tourists. The world's largest is the MGM Grand in Las Vegas, USA, with 5005 rooms.

◀ **Hotels began to use a system of stars in the 1830s to represent quality. A luxury hotel, such as the Ritz in London, England, shown here, will have five stars.**

Under canvas

Holiday camps range from a simple field where people can pitch a tent to enormous sites that are equipped with every kind of facility that a family could need on holiday.

The first children's summer camps were started in the USA in around 1885. They were designed to give children from the city a taste of country life. At first, they were only for boys. The first camps for girls started to appear at the end of the 19th century.

◀ **Kids' camps in the USA offer several weeks of activities throughout the school summer holidays.**

LOOK CLOSER

Camping has long been popular for holidays because tents offer a cheap and easy form of accommodation – all you need is a field to stay in. Modern tents make it even easier as some models are designed to 'pop' open using a spring-loaded frame.

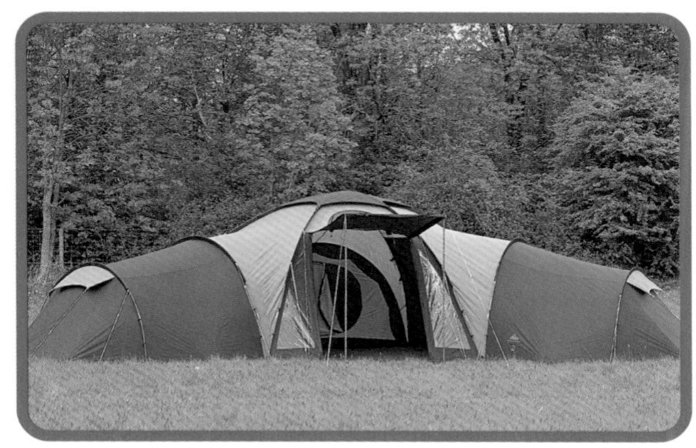

The first purpose-built holiday camp for adults was set up on the Isle of Man, UK, in 1894. It was just for men and offered very basic facilities. In contrast, modern camp sites can be found worldwide and offer a variety of facilities. Some even cater for specialist activities, such as tennis and maths tuition.

◀ **Modern holiday camps have restaurants, swimming pools and entertainment facilities. Some cover more than 160 hectares – that's about the size of 230 football pitches.**

Resorts

The 19th century saw the expansion of holiday resorts – purpose-built places that are designed to cater for the needs of holiday-makers. Today, there are beach resorts, as well as health and sporting resorts.

The earliest resorts were designed to improve a person's health. The spa waters at Bath in England were first used for their healing powers in 836 BC. During the 18th century, seaside towns became popular after doctors commented on the health benefits of seawater.

▼ Today, many people prefer to visit beach resorts in foreign countries. In 2003, UK residents made some 61.5 million journeys to foreign countries.

◀ Ski resorts offer accommodation, restaurants, bars and access to ski slopes via lifts and cable cars. The first cable car for skiers opened at the Swiss resort of Klosters in 1932.

As tourist numbers increased, so did the amount of money generated by tourism, and holiday resorts became an important part of every country's income. Today, the tourist industry creates some 318 billion pounds' worth of income worldwide each year.

LOOK CLOSER

Safaris are holidays where tourists can see wildlife in its natural setting. Safari lodges are built in national parks and nature reserves so that the tourists are near to the animals. Specialist guides advise and look after the tourists.

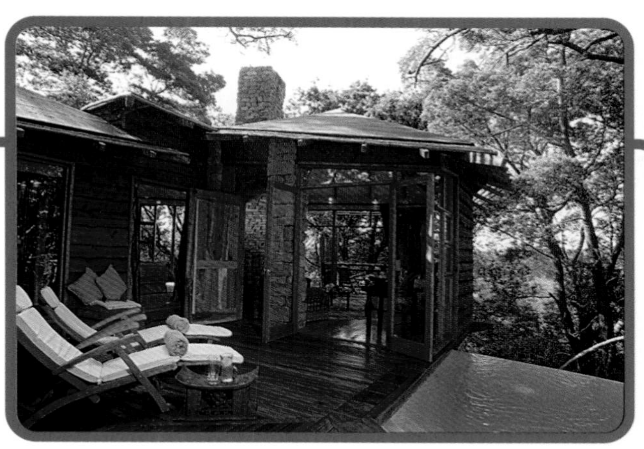

Boats and cruising

Travelling by boat used to be the quickest method of going to distant countries. Today, it has become a popular way to spend a holiday, with people cruising in vast liners, sailing in yachts or travelling along rivers in small boats.

When the steamship *Great Western* crossed the Atlantic Ocean in 1838, it took just 15 days, halving the time taken by sailing ships. After World War I (1914–18), the conversion of many warships into large passenger ships called liners helped to reduce the cost of cruising and make it more popular.

▼ By the 1920s, when this photo was taken, cruise liners could carry nearly 2500 people.

In recent years, the variety of boat holidays has increased. Large liners still cruise the oceans, while many holiday companies now run sailing holidays, where people can learn how to sail a yacht.

▲ Canal narrow boats, which once pulled cargo, have been converted into holiday boats for cruising canals and rivers.

LOOK CLOSER

Modern ocean liners are equipped with the most luxurious facilities. The *Queen Mary II* can carry 2620 passengers. Some of the rooms inside are fitted with their own private lift, two bathrooms and a balcony. There are also ten restaurants to choose from.

Rail travel

From the mid-19th century, regular train services gave holiday-makers easy access to resorts at home and abroad, and rail travel was available to both the rich and less wealthy. Modern trains still carry tourists on holiday, but at much greater speeds.

The expansion of rail networks in the last half of the 19th century linked large towns with resorts, while crossing entire continents. Local day trips became possible, and long, luxurious rail journeys were soon popular with the rich.

◀ The Orient Express train ran from Paris to Constantinople (now Istanbul). It started in 1883 and passengers travelled in luxury.

◀ The railway across the USA opened in 1869 and was the world's first transcontinental railway. Tourists can still travel this route in trains pulled by steam locomotives.

Competition from the plane and the car in the last half of the 20th century saw a decline in the use of rail travel. Even so, trains are still a popular method of travel and fast diesel and electric trains, such as the French TGV, carry thousands of tourists to destinations at more than 300 km/h.

EUREKA!

The earliest sleeping cars were introduced on US railways in 1836, but passengers had to bring their own bedding. The first rail coach that was specifically designed for comfortable night-time travel was created by George Pullman and Ben Field nearly 30 years later in 1865.

Motoring holidays

The increase in affordable cars changed how people travelled on holiday. New roads were laid to carry the greater number of road users, and vehicles were developed that allowed tourists to take their accommodation with them.

In 1909, Henry Ford introduced the world's first affordable motor car, the Model T. Suddenly, cars were available to millions of people, and many started to drive them to travel on holiday. Cars were used to pull caravans, and trucks were converted to create mobile homes.

▼ These motorists from the 1920s are eating their meal on the side of the road as there were few roadside facilities available for the driver.

Today, the car is an essential part of holiday travelling. About 80 per cent of all journeys are made by car, and holiday resorts take this into account. For example, Disneyland's California Adventure resort, which opened in 2001, was built with a car park big enough to hold 10 242 cars.

▲ This mobile home can sleep six people, with two people sleeping in the space above the driver's cab.

LOOK CLOSER

Caravans and mobile homes are equipped with all the appliances of a modern home. These include a fully fitted kitchen and washroom. The power to run all of these appliances comes from batteries or electrical supply points at a camp site.

Air travel

The plane revolutionised travel after the creation of the first airlines in 1919. Since then, it has allowed tourists to visit places that would have been difficult to reach in the past.

The first airlines used old military aircraft. Passengers had to wear thick clothes to stay warm and cotton wool in their ears to block out the engine noise. By the middle of the 1920s, standards had improved and airlines offered in-flight food and movies.

▼ Seaplanes and flying boats were used for flights from the 1920s. They could fly long distances in short hops from port to port.

▲ Also called the Jumbo Jet, the Boeing 747 can carry more than 500 people and travel for over 13 500 km without refuelling.

The first jet airliner was the de Haviland Comet, introduced in 1952. Jet airliners could fly farther and faster than propeller aircraft. As a result, air travel became cheaper and available to more people, allowing them to visit and experience foreign places and cultures.

LOOK CLOSER

Modern airports are enormous. The busiest is Hartsfield International Airport, Atlanta, USA, which serves over 80 million people every year, as well as handling their baggage. It has vast areas for runways and air-traffic control.

Travelling light

The travel industry has created a huge demand for a wide range of products and accessories to help the traveller. These include strong and light luggage, miniaturised electric devices and vaccinations to prevent disease.

As long ago as the 17th century, travellers were aware that certain substances could protect them from illness. Quinine, made from the bark of a tree, was noted for curing malaria in 1633. Today, there are vaccinations for a wide range of diseases, as well as chemical insect repellents and suntan creams.

▼ Early luggage consisted of wooden crates, leather cases or simple sacks. Modern luggage is made from artificial materials that are strong and light.

▼ This travel iron is just 19 cm long and weighs only 0.7 kg. Other miniaturised electric travel accessories include hair driers and kettles.

Many modern accessories are designed to be small and light to save space. Clothing that is specially designed for travellers is made from materials that are lightweight, easy to pack and quick drying.

EUREKA!

The first suntan cream appeared in 1936. It was called Ambre Solaire and was made by L'Oreal. Suntan creams protect against harmful rays from the sun and are available as cream, oil, spray, lotion or foam.

Paperwork

People can move freely around their country of birth, but they need official documents called passports in order to enter another country. These have photographs and information that identify the traveller.

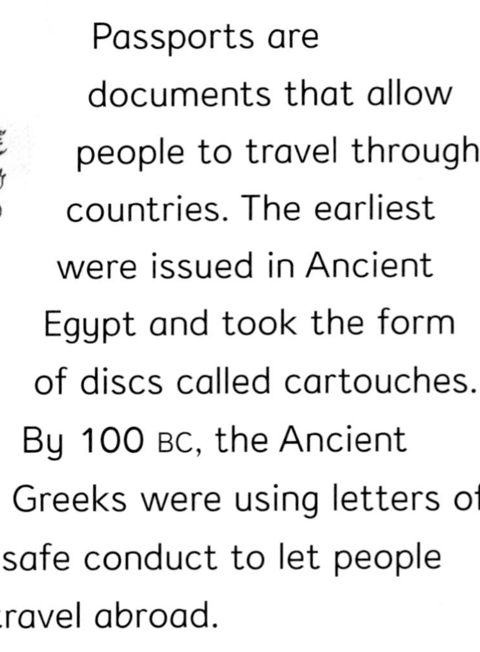

Passports are documents that allow people to travel through countries. The earliest were issued in Ancient Egypt and took the form of discs called cartouches. By 100 BC, the Ancient Greeks were using letters of safe conduct to let people travel abroad.

◀ The top passport is a simple sheet of paper. It was issued in 1837 to allow the Polish composer Chopin to visit Britain. In 1916, booklet passports, similar to those used today, were introduced.

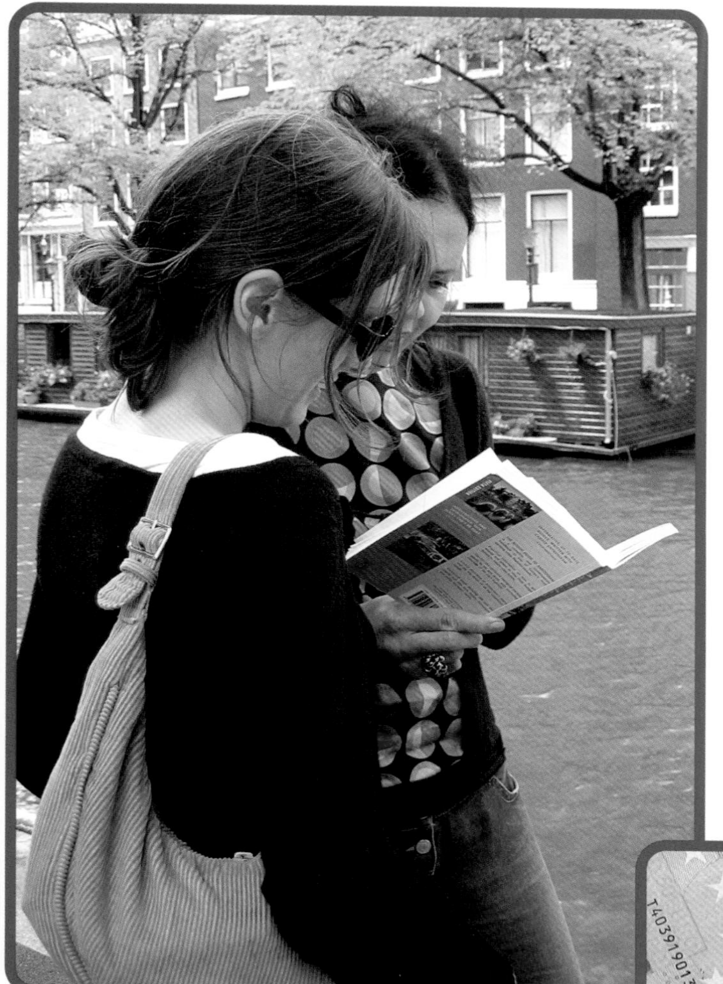

As well as a passport, many countries require travellers to apply for visas. These are documents that give permission to enter a country on a specific trip and for a set period of time. Threats to national security have also seen some countries demanding that passports are fitted with a computer chip. This will store unique identifying details about the traveller, such as fingerprints.

▲ **Publishers produce travel guides to help people find their way around. They became popular after German, Karl Baedeker, published his first guide in 1829.**

EUREKA!

In 1891, the American Express company introduced traveller's cheques. These allowed people to draw local currency while abroad. This reduced the amount of cash and foreign currency that people had to carry around with them.

Timeline

900 BC

• C.1836 BC. The hot-water spa in Bath, England, is visited for its healing powers.

• C.100 BC. The Ancient Greeks start to use letters of safe conduct as early passports.

• AD 117–138. Roman Emperor Hadrian builds a villa in Tivoli, Italy.

• C.1550. Young, wealthy men start touring the cities of Europe in what became known as the Grand Tour.

• 1633. Quinine is first used for its ability to cure malaria.

• 1829. Karl Baedeker publishes his first travel guide.

• C.1830. A star system is adopted to grade the quality of hotels.

• 1836. The first railway sleeping cars are introduced in the US.

• 1841. Thomas Cook starts to organise trips and sets up the world's first travel agency.

• 1865. George Pullman and Ben Field design the first purpose-built rail carriage with sleeping cabins.

• 1869. The world's first transcontinental railway opens in the USA.

• 1871. The South Metropolitan Gas Company gives its workers paid holidays.

• 1883. The first Orient Express train runs between Paris and Constantinople.

• c.1885. The first summer camps for children are started in the US.

• 1891. American Express release the first traveller's cheques.

• 1894. The first purpose-built camp for adults is opened on the Isle of Man, UK.

• 1909. Henry Ford introduces the Model T, the world's first affordable motor car.

• 1916. Booklet passports are introduced.

• 1919. The first airlines are formed.

• 1932. The world's first cable car for skiers opens in Klosters, Switzerland.

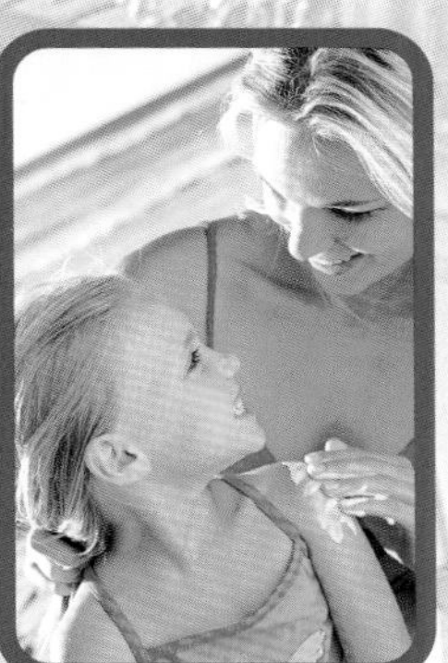

• 1936. Ambre Solaire makes the world's first suntan cream.

• 1952. The de Haviland Comet becomes the world's first jet-powered airliner.

• 1952. Kemmons Wilson opens the first Holiday Inn hotel.

• 1970. Boeing 747 Jumbo Jet enters service.

• 2004. Passports are introduced containing computer chips with information about the passport owner.

TODAY

Factfile

• The English word 'posh' comes from a term used to describe a type of ticket bought for people travelling between Great Britain and India in the 19th century. Wealthy travellers wanted the most comfortable cabins, and these were on the shaded side of the ship. On the journey out, these cabins were on the port side and on the starboard side for the journey back. People wanting these cabins would ask for a 'posh' ticket: Port Out, Starboard Home.

• The fastest jet airliner was the Tupolev Tu-144 from the Soviet Union. It could fly at 2587 km/h – that's nearly two-and-a-half times the speed of sound!

• The US has more airports than any other country, with 14 459. The next country is Brazil, which has 3291.

• The world's oldest hotel is the 100-room Hoshi Ryokan in Awazu, Japan. It dates back to AD 717 and was built near a hot-water spring that people visited for its healing powers.

• The world's busiest international air route is between Taipei in Taiwan and Hong Kong in China. Every year, nearly four million people fly this journey. The second-busiest international route is between London in the UK and Dublin in the Republic of Ireland.

Glossary

Backpacking
Travelling around without staying in one place for too long. It gets its name from the backpacks that people carry with them and use to store their clothes and possessions.

Currency
The money used in a particular country.

Motel
A roadside hotel that is designed to cater for motorists.

Narrow boat
A thin barge that was used to carry or pull industrial cargo along canals. Today, many of these boats have been converted into homes and pleasure boats.

Package holiday
A holiday where everything is arranged by a travel agent. This includes travel, accommodation and sometimes meals.

Passport
An official document or booklet that identifies a traveller and allows them to travel from one country to another.

Persian
A person from the ancient civilisation that flourished around 2500 years ago in the Middle East.

Pilgrimage
A journey that is made to a holy site for religious reasons.

Quinine
A chemical taken from the bark of the cinchona tree. Quinine has been used to fight the effects of the disease malaria.

Republic
A country in which the elected government is the highest power.

Travel agency
An organisation that arranges and books holidays for people.

Vaccination
A type of medicine, often injected, that protects a person against a certain disease.

Villa
A large house in the country. Roman villas were usually built around a pool of water, and indeed, today, many holiday villas have pools.

Index